Understanding
&
Building
Confidence

Other books available include:

Managing Stress & Preventing Depression

Motivation, Achievement & Challenges

Please make a donation if you can

TEXT: BOOK32£5

To: 70070

Or an online donation via:

www.justgiving.com/healthbooks

THANK YOU!

Understanding

&

Building

Confidence

by

Charlie Wardle

Climb Your
Mountain

Published under licence by Brown Dog Books and

The Self Publishing Partnership

7 Green Park Station, Bath BA1 1JB

www.selfpublishingpartnership.co.uk

ISBN: 978-1-903056-55-4

Cover design by Kevin Rylands

Printed and bound by CPI Group (UK) Ltd, Croydon CR0 4YY

Contents

About the author

Charlie Wardle set up the health and wellbeing charity Climb Your Mountain in 2008 and has since been running it in a full-time capacity ever since. Before founding Climb Your Mountain, Charlie had built a successful career in finance, qualified as a chartered accountant, obtained an MBA from a top Business School and, in his last role before setting up the charity, became the Finance Director of a large global publishing company.

During the last few years Charlie has carried out extensive research into many areas of health and wellbeing including stress, depression, anxiety, confidence, motivation, exercise and nutrition. He has delivered hundreds of talks, workshops and courses over the last few years on these topics and his insight and knowledge is a combination of his own experiences, meeting and talking to hundreds of people and the extensive research covered.

His passion is providing opportunities for people to improve their physical and mental health and to become happier. Those opportunities provided include a series of health and wellbeing books to read, a range of courses and workshops to attend and numerous physical activities, trips and challenges to participate in with the charity.

Twitter: @CYMCharlie   Email: info@climbyourmountain.org

Introduction

Confidence – *the anticipation of a positive outcome*
(and if the outcome is not positive, knowing you can deal with it!)

Our levels of confidence will affect us in our daily lives in all kinds of different ways. Those confidence levels affect our work, our relationships, friendships, fitness, health, thinking, beliefs, actions, attitude, behaviours and our happiness.

The vast majority of people would like to be more confident and certainly nobody would want to feel less confident than they do. So if most people want to be more confident that would imply that there is an issue that really should be addressed. So here is my effort in trying to help people increase their confidence, and the most important thing is for people to understand what confidence means to them in the first place! Secondly, and equally as important, is practice... but we will come to that later in the book.

In order to develop your own confidence you need to understand confidence, both the general understanding and also your own personal understanding, as this can often differ considerably. Your perception of confidence, your own and other people's, could be very different from how someone else sees it and what the main factors are related to your differing perspectives.

So we need to hear from different people, look at different factors, understand different elements and then bring these all together so that you have a much better understanding of confidence. Once you understand confidence you are then in a much better place actually to start building your own confidence and becoming a more confident and self-assured person.

I believe there is always an explanation for how someone behaves and thinks. The key is to try and understand the reasons behind those thoughts and actions. With regard to confidence, work out why you don't feel confident and then look at how best to address these areas in the most effective way. Work out what the key factors are and seek to put in place plans to overcome, prevent, discard, build upon, reframe or change them.

The first half of this book really looks at understanding confidence and the second half looks at how you can then improve your confidence using a range of tools, techniques and practical tips, re-enforcing the need to practice and keep working at it. The more you understand, the easier it is to build the confidence by practising the techniques. The more you practise, the more confident you get and the more confident you get the easier it is to maintain.

> **'Whether you think you can or you can't, you will (most probably) be right.'** – *Henry Ford*

I love this quote from Henry Ford. It is so true that your beliefs and thought processes are so important to the results you achieve in life. Your chances of success and getting the result you want are greatly improved if you think that will happen and conversely the chances are greatly diminished if you think you can't achieve the results you want.

A recent example that highlights this for me was on a weekend group trip to Snowdon run by the Climb Your Mountain charity. It was a relatively small group of people which included a mix of new people and a few more experienced participants who had attended our trips before. I was introducing people to each other on the Saturday morning and one of the new ladies immediately said how she was hopeless with names and would never remember anyone. As people often do, she said it in a half joking way and quickly repeated again how she could never remember people's names and was useless at that kind of thing.

Later in the day, I asked a few people in the group if they had remembered everyone's names and did a few quick tests at random. Once again, the same lady quickly said how she was rubbish with names and wouldn't be able to remember, claiming she had always been useless with names. We continued with the day but at dinner in the evening I was seated next to this lady and after a while I raised the subject of the names of other people in the group. Again she reiterated how bad she was with names, always had been and she was useless at anything like that.

I asked her if she would try, just for a couple of minutes, forgetting about how bad she was and instead believe she could do it and just focus on each member of the group. Within a few minutes she had remembered everyone's names and she was visibly quite shocked and surprised that she had done this.

For nearly all her life she had immediately put up a barrier with the belief she couldn't do this task. She had no confidence at all in her ability to remember names. She believed she wouldn't be able to remember so she didn't. Most likely she had experienced something when she was younger that knocked her confidence in this way and made her feel like she couldn't do this or similar tasks. Also likely was that someone else had told her this was the case, and with absolute certainty she herself had reinforced this negative belief continually ever since.

This belief and attitude will only ever remain and become even more fixed if it is not addressed. However, it was proven within a few short minutes that she wasn't useless and she could remember the names with a little focus and effort. So going forward in any similar situation, her instinct needs to be that she can rather than she can't. This will require practice as such an ingrained belief can be difficult to change, but it can change and with that change a greater confidence can be gained.

No longer does she have to put up that barrier and hold that negative belief about herself. In so many cases people will have these false barriers and beliefs due to past experiences or people telling them they can't do something. The reality is that in many cases the person can and when they think and believe they can, then they will!

Questionnaires

Over the last year I have run several 'confidence' workshops and the attendees were asked to complete a short questionnaire beforehand with a list of questions relating to confidence. Below are a range of responses to some of the questions asked. It is often helpful to show other people's views and perceptions, so that you may recognise some of the common traits.

What is your definition of confidence?

- *Feeling self-assured – having self-belief and faith in yourself. Not questioning yourself all the time, not doubting yourself. Being established in life and feeling capable and competent.*

- *Not having 'the fear of failure' sitting on your shoulder. Being able to say what you feel/believe without the fear of being wrong or appearing idiotic.*

- *Being comfortable with who you are and resilient to negative influences. To be comfortable in your own skin and to be able to express yourself openly.*

- *Being able to talk or put forward your opinion on something to others in any given situation (i.e. in a one-on-one conversation, in a small group or on a much larger scale, say as part of a presentation or talk) without hesitation. Believing in yourself enough that you are sure of what you are saying and doing.*

- *It's having the ability to talk to anyone in any situation. Daring to do something different and out of your comfort zone.*

- *I would describe it as the ability to project and feel good in yourself, with what you do and how you do it. Being assertive and able to get a point or opinion across. Not feeling awkward or lost.*

- *To me it's the ability to stand up for yourself and your beliefs, and the ability to make others believe them too.*

- *The ability to do things you want without worrying about what other people might think. Being happy with yourself and comfortable in who you are. Believing in yourself and your decisions.*

- *Being at ease with one's self and beliefs, able to overcome self-doubt, able to live as I want to rather than how people expect me to be.*

What are the characteristics/behaviours of a confident person?

- *Self-belief, no hesitancy with own opinions, stop looking to others for reassurance, individuality, unafraid to walk alone i.e. not follow the crowd.*

- *Characteristics are being positive, assertive, have self-belief and happy with their abilities. Their behaviours are being able to communicate well with presentation skills, with a professional image and being able to take the lead.*

- *Someone who is able to chat to others whatever the situation, who is not afraid to speak up and is able to say what they think in a convincing way or to get their point across clearly without sounding arrogant. Someone who doesn't care if they look stupid if they say or do something wrong.*

- *Open body language, holding their head up high, speaking clearly, maintaining eye-contact with the person they're speaking to, relaxed shoulders and body posture.*

- *I think the characteristics and behaviours are that they are fearless of what others think and they are prepared to take risks. I believe that someone's background, including upbringing, experiences and self-perception is what makes someone confident.*

- *They appear sure of themselves and in their abilities. They may come across as bubbly or direct. They may be chatty and able to tackle new things more easily. I believe an inner belief in one's self would make a person more confident.*

- *Someone who is confident projects a high self-esteem, is happy to celebrate success* and accept compliments, but equally is able to hold their hand up and admit a mistake and change course. Confident people are positive and transformational in their thinking; barriers are there to be overcome ,not to block their way.

- Happy, sociable, out-going, focused, organised, decisive self-belief and the ability to react well to knock-backs. Someone that looks at ease and can converse easily with anyone at any level.

- Confident people are not afraid to speak their mind; they behave in a way which tells everyone around that they're decisive and that they can be trusted.

- They are happy and comfortable with themselves. They aren't concerned about what other people think about them, and they don't compare themselves to other people.

- Animated, warm open nature. By inspiring others with their behaviour I think this must help re-enforce positive feeling

What do you fear? What do you worry about?

- Going out to work and holding it together. Not being able to get a job (contradictory with first item). Being found out to be incompetent / a fraud. Being tired. Beating myself up about my capabilities.

- Talking in a large group of people. Saying the wrong thing – feeling stupid. Upsetting people – worrying about what people think. Money and security.

- Looking like a fool in front of other people. Lack of control, being in a situation that's out of my comfort zone.

- I have quite a strong fear of social situations and interaction with others. Not a confident conversationalist. I hate having focus put on me, dislike even being on camera or hearing my own voice played back. I have always had a sense of being a bit 'odd' and not fitting in or belonging in groups of people so tend to withdraw when I'm feeling at my most vulnerable.

- *To be housebound, maybe immobile with illness and not able to be out and about. I am fearful of loneliness. Worrying is a bit out of balance for me at the moment. Worry is related to my anxiety. Worry that I may never understand 'how to fully help myself' and manage my mental health problems. It is a long journey. I have to move forward and the steps I take are so small.*

- *I worry about being alone. I fear death and ill health in general. I worry about doing something wrong at work. I fear rejection. I worry about what other people think of me and upsetting other people. That something I have said will have upset someone. I worry that when I do talk I am misunderstood and inadvertently upset people. That I will fail if I try to do something new. I worry about the fact I am quiet around small groups of friends and it has been commented on. I worry about how nothing I do seems to go the way I would like it to. I worry about everything; if I have nothing to worry about I will find something.*

- *Feeling pain emotionally, what other people think of me, making a mistake, failure, going into the unknown (networking, interviews, first time situations), situations I can't control (flying).*

- *I fear change and I do not like to feel unsettled. Work causes me a lot of worry and makes me unhappy at times. What people think of me worries me, even if they say positive things about/to me I still doubt.*

- *I fear that I haven't achieved enough in a work sense, I fear that I should be doing so much more and that I might one day be 'found out'. I worry that if I put myself forward and have to take hard decisions that I will become unpopular. I feel that I veer erratically from being overly cynical to being naive and worry that this makes me withdraw my participation socially and so keep my guard up.*

- *Worry that someone wouldn't like me and that I can be socially awkward. Financial issues stopping me doing things I like. Putting on weight and feeling unattractive.*

- *I fear being unhappy. I worry about what will happen in my life, my job, relationships etc. I am worried that I am not making the most of my life. I also worry about bad things happening to my family and friends, illnesses, death etc.*

Why would you like to be more confident?

- *So I can get the old me back.*

- *So I can be happy with myself and my life. I would like to be able to think more positively and not be so down about myself. Would also hopefully like to meet people who feel the same as me so I don't feel like the shy odd one out.*

- *I suppose I am mostly thinking on a personal level that I want to be able to open up to new people, to follow up meeting people with a phone call. My children will be leaving home in the next few years and I want to move into a new life phase with new aims.*

- *I would like to get back the confidence I used to have because life was so much easier/better that way. I believe I will be much happier and accepting, I will stop worrying. I will get back the motivation and concentration to study and learn. I will clear my mind of all the things that I worry about now and I will focus on setting and achieving goals.*

- *I want to overcome my fear of attending parties and social functions. I need to get out of a rut and make a push to change direction in my life. Expand my network and meet new people.*

- *I would like to be more confident as I currently feel that my lack of self-confidence in my abilities and what I have to offer could restrict my progression at work. I would like to understand the causes of low confidence and how they may relate to me but, importantly, also work on a programme or 'tool-set' to overcome the innate self-doubt and promote the confidence in my abilities that other people seem to have.*

- *I would like to be more confident in order to live my life in a happier and settled way with true belief in myself. Being less negative, I feel, would help me be more confident. I would like to find a belief in myself at these workshops and be able to explore what would make me more confident and happy. I would also like to stop the negativity which seems to have always been a big part of my life.*

- *I believe not feeling confident is actually affecting me physically and emotionally every day of my life and has done for many years. I want to feel better about myself and strong enough to go ahead and achieve some of the things I've always wanted to.*

- *I want to be more confident so I am able to sit with a group of friends and not have all the things I want to say going round my head but being unable to say them out loud and join in the conversation. I want to believe in myself again, enough that I can put myself forward for new jobs and not worry about the rejections and to be confident enough to sell myself in the applications and interviews, not constantly doubting myself. I want to be able to initiate conversations with people without the turmoil I currently feel if I am asked to go and talk to someone.*

- *To be able to impress at an interview and be successful in changing my job if I choose to. To be more easily heard and understood, enjoy the company of others without being anxious.*

- *I want to feel like I believe that people value what I say. I want to feel that I can make a difference. I want to learn new ideas and/or receive reinforcement of existing ideas that will enable/assist me in the process of validating my opinion/input.*

- *To gain inner confidence and self-belief. To be able to sell myself in an interview to get a great job that I love. Not to worry so much about what people think.*

- *Survival! Need to be self-assured and stop self-sabotaging. Stop beating myself up. Be optimistic and have faith in myself. Make life easier for others around me.*

Conclusion and summary of questionnaires

The selection of answers and comments from people shows both a wide range of views and also some strong common themes. Many of the above comments and words will probably resonate with you and hopefully they have been useful in your own thinking and how you would respond to the same questions.

Take some time to think about your answers, or even better, write them down so you have them documented and you can refer back when appropriate. This process will help you think in more depth about your own confidence and help you focus on the key areas that need working on. Be completely open and honest with yourself, and although it may be quite difficult and emotional it will help you to both understand and then build your confidence.

'We have to learn to be our own best friend because we fall too easily into the trap of being our own worst enemy.' – *Roderick Thorp*

Part 1

Understanding Confidence

'The greatness of a man is not in how much wealth he acquires, but in his integrity and his ability to affect those around him positively' – Bob Marley

Your values, identity and integrity

Before going into more detail about understanding confidence it is essential that you consider your own values, identity and integrity as they are fundamental to who you are, what you want from your life, how you deal with situations and how you react to people. Everyone is different and this is a result of nature, nurture, circumstances and experiences; everyone will have their own values, identity and integrity as a result. These values are core to that individual and to be true to yourself you must stick with these values to maintain your own identity, integrity and beliefs. If you stray from these values, for whatever reason, then you are likely to feel worse about yourself and lose your integrity, and as a result your confidence could be affected.

So take time to understand yourself and who you are. A great story that highlights this is from the most sacred place in the ancient world, the oracle at Delphi in central Greece. Kings, warriors and envoys travelled from across the known world to hear the prophecies of the oracle. Above the gates at Delphi, a short inscription greeted every weary traveller: **Know thyself**. This simple advice was considered the most important piece of knowledge anyone could possess. And to understand what the oracle told you, you first had to understand yourself.

You may find yourself in difficult positions, perhaps due to other people, financial issues, relationships, stress, depression, work problems, drink or drugs, where you find yourself compromising your own core values. Whether you want to admit to it or not, you will be aware, and the further away you stray from your core values the worse your situation is likely to become.

It is important that no matter what is happening in your life you can retain your values and integrity so that you are able to look yourself in the mirror and know that you are being true to yourself and true to your values. Life will always throw you curve balls; some people will always let you down, have a different view, misunderstand the situation, etc. and there will always be some issues to deal with in life. We just need to teach ourselves how best to deal with these issues and challenges.

One of the best ways to understand your own core values is to ask yourself what matters most in your life, what are the most important things and what characteristics in people do you respect the most? Take some time to really work out what is important to you and look to define and document these core values.

Something else that can be helpful is to think about a person or people whom you admire and respect the most – whether that is someone you know personally or perhaps a famous name you look up to. Then consider what it is about them that you really admire and respect. What is it about their behaviour, actions, words, achievements, etc. that you hold in high regard? Maybe it's their courage, determination, resilience, honesty, etc. It is quite likely that your core values and what you see as truly important are very similar to what you recognise, admire and respect in that other person.

Knowing the real you and having your own identity is really important in order to retain your values and integrity. Often people will lose their way, no longer sure of who they are, living a life for others rather than their own life and not feeling like the real them any more.

So spend time understanding the real you, knowing your core values, having your own identity and always maintaining your integrity. These are fundamental foundations for your health and happiness in general and very specifically for your own self-confidence.

   'It's not the mountain we conquer, but ourselves.'

Confidence factors – the 8 main categories

'Nothing in life is to be feared. It is only to be understood.'

Confidence can be quite complex and is based upon many factors which will differ from person to person. In order to increase your confidence it is vital that you look at as many of these factors as possible and try to understand how they apply to you. I have broken down these confidence factors into eight main categories as follows:

Within each category there will be many things to think about, to consider, to understand, to work on and to apply to yourself. Remember, everybody is different, an individual, and you need to be honest with yourself and really take time to drill down on each area. Some areas will be more relevant and more important than others and there will be some quick wins as well as some more difficult, longer-term factors to work on.

By breaking down all the factors and understanding them you will be in a much better position to build up your confidence and sustain it in the long run.

The 8 Factors in detail

YOU

You must look carefully at yourself and your understanding of confidence. Think about who you are, your values, your strengths, your weaknesses, your personality, your beliefs, your perceptions, your skills, your thoughts and your behaviours. Be reflective, patient and honest with yourself but realise you are the most important person in your life, and your attitude and the way you see yourself are key.

> *'When we change our attitude towards ourselves, everything else changes as well, for our life is a reflection of the way we feel inside'* – Dr Mansukh Patel

What do you think about yourself?

The most important thing regarding confidence is yourself and what you think of yourself. These thoughts will be based on a wide mix of factors including your genetics, your upbringing, your family, people who have influenced your life (in both good and bad ways), your friends, your job, your health, your looks, your body, your experiences (both positive and negative) and much more. Often what you think about yourself will be very different from how other people view you and although you should know yourself better than anyone, your views of yourself could be influenced by many external factors and may be distorted.

There is a great quote that goes 'Whether you think you can, or you think you can't, you will most likely be right'... and in a way this is the same when you think about yourself. Confidence is ultimately how you think or feel about yourself, so in order to be more confident and feel confident you must be able to think positively about yourself and work at being a 'better' you from your own perspective.

Your perception on things, beliefs, thoughts

Although basing things on facts is very important and wherever possible you should base decisions, thoughts, behaviours and actions on facts, the reality is that your confidence is based upon your perception of things and not always based on facts. So your perception of yourself, of others, of experiences, of information, etc. is key to your confidence.

You should aim to close the gap between perception and facts where you can but this is not always possible and also can be very difficult. Try to be rational and reflective and consider all factors. Not everything you hear, see or believe will be true, so be careful not to jump to conclusions, or make too many assumptions or judgements without being certain they are correct

Self-assurance, self-esteem, self-confidence

How self-assured are you? How would you rate your self-esteem? How would you describe your self-confidence? It is important to think about this, but ask yourself how you are personally measuring this. What are your criteria? What are you basing your views on? Are you comparing yourself against others and if so, who? Have you always felt like this or are you comparing yourself to the past? If you feel differently now to times in the past then what has changed? What are the factors and reasons? By asking yourself these questions and thinking about it you are likely to have a more complete and balanced view and an improved awareness of the factors that have shaped your opinions.

Your attitude, your past, your understanding

Experiences throughout your life will shape your views and so will your understanding of these experiences and your attitude. Many events, situations, people, and circumstances will have contributed to who you are, how you think, how you behave and how you feel about yourself, which, of course, impacts on your confidence. Understanding how they have impacted you and your ability to deal with them will play a key role in both how you currently feel and how you can move forward with developing your confidence.

Your attitude is key to this and needs to be looked at in detail. Do you want to improve? Do you believe you can improve? Are you willing to make the effort and changes needed to have a more confident and happier life? By wanting to read this book you have acknowledged a lack of self-belief and are now on the way to improving your confidence and your life greatly.

> *'A bird sitting on a tree is never afraid of the branch breaking, because its trust is not on the branch but on its own wings.'*

OTHERS

You will always be influenced by other people in life, in both good ways and bad. You cannot control other people, but you can control the effect they have on you and how you think and behave towards others. With the right people and the right attitude your confidence will increase significantly. The hard part is ensuring you have the right people in your life and working out how you deal with and react to all of the people that enter your life at different times.

> *'No one can make you feel inferior without your consent'* – *Eleanor Roosevelt*

Why do you worry what people think?

Pretty much everyone, to some extent, worries about what other people think of them. So if you are someone who worries what people think then you are not alone, and to some degree it can be a good thing that you care what others do think about you. However, far too often the worrying about what people think can be damaging, negative and stressful. It will very often lower confidence, cause anxiety and restrict you from doing things, and can lead to health issues.

Worrying that people might not like you, might think you are stupid, might laugh at you, might reject you, etc. are all common and negative concerns which can be detrimental to your confidence

Do they really think that of you? Would you think like that of others?

Most of the time the concern and worry of what others are thinking is simply not a reality. Are people really judging you as you believe they are and hoping to dislike you or laugh at you? Are they willing you to do something stupid or fail? Are they thinking how much better they are than you? Most of the time the answer is definitely no! People you don't really know are normally not that interested and those people you know as friends or family are going to be supportive and be thinking positively and encouraging you.

When you see or meet people for the first time are you looking to put them down, laugh at them, dislike them, think they are stupid, etc.? Think about situations where you worry what people are thinking and turn it around to see how you would be thinking in that situation. Would you be so harsh and critical? I suspect the answer is no, and that is how most people will be.

Other people have issues, problems, insecurities, etc.

It is very easy to focus just on yourself and any particular issues, worries, insecurities, doubts and low confidence you may be experiencing. However, other people have these, too! Yes, you are not the only one who worries and thinks and behaves your way. Many people will be struggling with worse issues and disorders that affect their behaviour and thinking. So be mindful that other people have issues and what you see and get may be down to that. For example, if someone is a bit cold and distant with you upon meeting you and you take that to mean they don't like you and it must be something bad about you, then consider it could be they are nervous, lacking confidence, worried about things, introverted, etc.; a whole range of possibilities in addition to the one you are focusing on.

Also, many of the seemingly most confident people are very insecure with low confidence, low self-esteem and high anxiety, but they cover it up or their way of dealing with it is to put on the front you see. Never judge a book by its cover!

Why let people cause you negativity, put you down, make you feel worse?

A lot of issues people have with confidence will come either directly or indirectly from other people. So often there will be people in your life, past and present, who will be a negative influence, will put you down, will make you feel worse and will be chipping away at your confidence and self-esteem. They could be partners, family members, work colleagues or so-called friends. Sometimes you will be aware of who they are and what they are doing but sometimes you may not even realise unless you actually step back and reflect on things and, by then, the damage has been done, the arrow has found its mark.

Of course, the answer is to stop this happening by either removing them from your life or confronting them. However, this can be very difficult and especially difficult if you are struggling with a lack of confidence. Think how you can minimise the negative impact others are having on you. Can you ignore them, can you confront them, could you take them out of your life? Can you be strong enough to accept their opinion but not let it affect you? The more you can minimise the damage caused to you the better.

> *'There comes a time when you have to stop crossing oceans for the people who wouldn't even jump puddles for you.'*

FEARS/WORRIES

As humans we are born with only two fears – the fear of falling and the fear of loud noise. So, apart from these, all our fears that we have are learned fears, either through someone telling us we should be fearful or from negative experiences that have affected and influenced us.

Fear of failure and fear of rejection

Two of the most common fears we have are the fear of failure and the fear of rejection, which are often closely linked. Nobody likes to fail or be rejected, but why do we fear and worry about these so much? The reality is that everyone will fail and be rejected at times during their life. It will happen. So rather than worrying and being fearful we should accept the inevitable and focus on how we deal with it. How can we learn, understand, grow, become stronger, change if necessary and use the experience in a positive way? The more confident you are the less you fear failure and rejection because you are confident that you can deal with the outcome. That is the difference and that should be where the focus is – on how you deal with it, rather than the fear beforehand.

Fear of feeling stupid

Another common fear is that you will do or say something that makes you look stupid. People worry that they won't be able to do something, or not do it correctly or embarrass themselves in some way. Again, the reality is that we all make mistakes, we all do things that will make us look stupid, and nobody is perfect.

Of course, you can try to minimise the risk in a number of ways, but if you simply stop doing things or saying things because of this fear then you will deprive yourself of so many things and so many opportunities in life. Your confidence will most likely decrease further as you stop being involved, withdraw more from conversations, events and activities and thus deny yourself the experiences that will help increase your confidence. Learn to laugh at yourself if you do say or do something stupid! Accept you will make mistakes; be honest and humble enough to apologise if needed and accept that you will, on occasions, look foolish, because that is life.

Fear of what others think

A basic human characteristic is the desire and need to be liked and loved. To feel wanted, to feel support and security, to feel that people care and to feel you have some kind of purpose. Humans are also inherently social creatures and like to have contact with others and be part of groups. So these basic characteristics make it likely and common that we will care about what others think of us and we will want to look good and be well thought of by others. It is normal to care about this and to think about it but this does not mean you should be in fear and constantly worrying about what others think. There is a big difference between being self-aware and caring about something, and being in fear.

Nervous, anxious, scared

It is likely that the lower your confidence the more you will feel nervous, anxious and scared in more situations. In turn the more you feel like this the lower your confidence becomes, so it becomes a negative virtuous circle. Most of the worry is effectively habitual and you become used to feeling like this. It is often irrational, too. It is important firstly to recognise the worry and then try to step back and rationalise the situation and try to put things into perspective.

It may be helpful to talk through the worry with a friend or think about what advice you would give a friend if the roles were reversed. Keep rationalising the situation and try to realise that the worry is not helping you. Try to focus on the reality and the positives of the situation. The more you do this the less you will worry and it will become more habitual not to feel so anxious, nervous and scared. More often than not, people with low confidence begin to develop irrational fears, so it is really important that you are able to recognise these fears and banish them from your mind. Irrational fears are not rational fears!

> *'You can never cross the ocean unless you have the courage to lose sight of the shore.'*

ACHIEVEMENT

As humans we need to have both purpose and fulfilment in our lives. This can be achieved in many different ways, but essentially we need to have things to strive for and achieve in life. With achievement there is a purpose that will give you fulfilment and in turn results in more happiness and increased confidence. Achievement builds confidence and the more confident we are the more we achieve, so this becomes a very positive virtuous circle.

What would you like to do? Why don't you do it?

Have you ever thought about something you would like to do and like to achieve but have never done? Of course you have, but what are the reasons for not doing these things? Are they genuine reasons or really just excuses? Some things may not be possible or realistic, but there will be many things that are not done due to factors that are simply excuses. As the saying goes 'If you want something, you will find a way. If not, you will find an excuse.' Think about how important something is to you, the rewards, the benefits, the achievement, and then work out if the effort, sacrifice, time, money, etc. is worth it. If yes, the answer is to stop making excuses and go for it. Life is for living, not just existing, so draw up a plan and put steps in place to make it happen.

The best feeling in the world is pride/achievement

Pride and achievement can come in many forms, but I would suggest that these feelings are the most rewarding and satisfying a person can have in their life, whether it's the pride in yourself for something you have done and achieved or whether it's pride for someone else like your child or partner achieving something amazing. Whatever the goal or challenge is, there will be a sense of pride in what you have achieved which equates to a powerful combination of purpose and fulfilment. The effort, the obstacles, the sacrifices, the pain, the time and the commitment all become worth it with the achievement and usually the harder something is to achieve the greater the sense of pride and the stronger the feeling.

The more you do the more confident you can become

As with most things, the more you do of something the better you get and in turn the more confident you become. And the more confident you become the more likely you are to try new experiences, set new goals and challenges, find new opportunities and in turn further your confidence even more. Focus on setting yourself goals, targets, challenges in all kinds of ways and make the effort, find the time, commit to them and your confidence will soar when they are achieved. You may need help, support, advice, encouragement, motivation, etc., especially to start with, so don't be afraid to ask and seek this help. Before long you will be the one helping and inspiring others!

Be careful if you fail and how you might react

There is every possibility that you could fail in any attempt to achieve a goal and you should give this some consideration before embarking on it. You should never fear failure but you should make sure your goals are realistic and achievable. You cannot possibly be successful in everything, so failure is inevitable, but how this affects you depends on your reaction and how you deal with the failure or perceived failure. If you have tried your hardest and given it your best shot then no matter the outcome you should feel proud. You cannot do better than your best! If you do fail then use it as a positive, to learn from it, to motivate you or to reassess expectations. It may fire you up to push even harder next time or you may need to learn to let something go and know when enough is enough. Sometimes, circumstances are stacked against us; for example, the weather or an injury, which leads us to not completing the task, so don't berate yourself if you're affected by things beyond your control.

'Nothing builds self-esteem and self-confidence like accomplishment.'

SELF-IMAGE

How we feel about ourselves is obviously very important to our confidence concerning both our physical and mental attributes. Our looks, our body shape, our fitness, our general health are all important on the physical side, whereas on the mental side factors like how interesting we are, how funny and how intelligent, are important, too, and all contribute to our confidence levels. Some of these factors are out of your control and are simply a result of your genetics, but many can be understood better and improved upon and thus help to increase your confidence.

How do I look?

How comfortable do you feel about your looks? Do you feel attractive? Does this change depending on different factors? Are you concerned about your looks and do you spend time worrying about this? How much effort do you make with your looks? Do you feel self-conscious about your looks or particular features? When do you feel at your best and your worst with regards to your looks? Concentrate on your best features and tell yourself, when you look in the mirror 'I have great teeth' or 'I love my hair' or 'my eyes are my greatest asset'. By reaffirming that you like something about yourself, you are on the first steps to building self-confidence.

Physical appearance

Are you happy and content with your physical appearance and body shape? Does this bother you at all? Do you consider yourself to be overweight or underweight? Are you concerned at all about your height? Are you happy with your clothes and the effort you make with your outward appearance? Most people will not like the way they look and their confidence levels can vary quite a lot depending on how they feel about their physical appearance. If, for example, someone is wearing a new outfit and has just been to the hairdressers then they might feel more confident as they like the new look. On the other hand if someone has put on weight and perhaps their skin is in a poor state they may feel less confident as a result.

How interesting am I?

Many people with low confidence will find it difficult to interact and be vocal in social situations and this will be more likely if they feel they are not interesting and don't have much to say. If you feel that you are not interesting or people won't want to listen to you or you haven't got much to say then this will make you become more withdrawn and less confident. You may be worried that people will think you are boring as well as quiet, so you may take yourself out of social situations or overly worry about upcoming events.

How intelligent am I?

Nobody wants to look or feel foolish or would want other people to think they are stupid. However, many people believe they are not very intelligent and as a result their confidence is diminished. Of course, everyone's natural intelligence varies and our education, upbringing, opportunities and circumstances will have a huge effect, but many people will put themselves down unfairly and think they are less intelligent than others. If you find yourself thinking or saying that you aren't very clever then you need to think about the negative effect of this and not let it affect your confidence.

'Be who you are and say what you feel, because those who mind don't matter, and those who matter don't mind.'

SECURITY

Feeling secure in your life is a nice, comforting feeling to have and will inherently add to your confidence in the same way that if you feel insecure then your confidence will decrease. People will look at security in a number of different ways and often will get things out of perspective. Think about what security means to you and how you can feel more secure about your surroundings, circumstances and, most importantly, secure within yourself.

Not just about what we don't have – but what we do have

It is all too easy to dwell on what we don't have in life and many people will be constantly thinking about what they would like to have. So these two thoughts combining the things we don't have and the things we want to have can be very negative and very unproductive. It is far better and more productive to think about the positives of what you do have. You will have a lot more than you realise and spending time thinking about all the good things you have will help put things into perspective and likely give you some additional assurance and security. Make a list of the positive attributes in your life and remind yourself frequently about the things that make your smile.

Money, job, partner, family, house, health

It is common for people to focus on particular elements of security like financial security and not consider other important areas. Security could be with your job, your partner, your family, your house, your health and many other things. Would you prefer financial security but poor health and no family? Do you underestimate the security your partner gives you or that of owning your own property? There are probably areas that do provide you with security but you rarely think about them and instead focus on the negative areas that make you feel insecure.

Be realistic about the situation and get things in perspective

It is really important to get life into perspective and be realistic. Understand the real difference between 'need' and 'want' and the reasons behind them. Do not neglect all the positives that can provide security and all of the opportunities to come which will bring greater security for you. Remember, things could always be worse, so count your blessings and be careful not to get things out of perspective.

Being secure in yourself is most important

You have to feel secure in yourself and believe in yourself. Security provides confidence and in turn confidence helps make you feel more secure, so belief in yourself is key. Strip away the negative thinking, the jealousy, the comparisons, the focus on what you don't have and instead concentrate on all the positive things you have and all the good things in your life. The more you focus on the positives the more you will gain belief in yourself and you will look forward and gain momentum in that belief.

> *'Too many people overvalue what they are not and don't have and undervalue what they are and do have.'*

HOPE/OPTIMISM

You are more likely to feel confident if you are a hopeful and optimistic person, thinking forward more positively with a glass half full approach to life. If you are pessimistic, thinking the worse, being negative and often looking backwards then your confidence is likely to suffer as a result. Generally the more confident you are, the more optimistic and vice versa. Optimism is generally a state of mind over which you have some control. You can choose to be more optimistic and hopeful with your attitude and thus it makes sense that if you do this then your confidence is likely to increase. Think about the people in your life who make you happy and distance yourself from those who don't – people who undermine you and your confidence and belittle you should have no room in your life.

Thinking positively

Life will always throw stuff at us that we don't like, don't want to deal with and don't want to happen and of course, life is not fair. However, by being pessimistic and negative, things will not improve and it will become harder to deal with life's challenges. By thinking positively and choosing to have that positive mindset you are making improvements to the situation. You are making a positive difference and even if that's all you are able to do, then choosing to think positively will be beneficial. Plus, the brain can only think one thought at a time, so make it a positive one!

Things to look forward to

It is also really important to look forward positively and this will be helped by thinking of things that you will look forward to. Things that you wish to do, places to go, people to see, skills to learn, challenges to achieve, etc., are all positive, forward-looking things that create an optimistic and hopeful mindset which in turn helps to boost confidence.

Things to smile about and feel good about

It is great when we feel happy, feel good about things and smile. So take opportunities to think about examples of what does make you smile and feel good. Which events, people, activities, experiences have made you feel good? What and whom makes you smile? Think about how you can have more of these experiences and make the effort to do more things that will make you smile, that you will enjoy and feel good about. Look at photographs to reaffirm that you have had great times in your life. Holiday photos are always a pleasure to look at, and ones of you smiling, having fun and making memories are a positive boost to your confidence. The more you do, the more confident you will feel.

Hope is the best of things

There is a quote from one of my favourite films (The Shawshank Redemption) that goes 'Hope is a good thing, maybe the best of things, and no good thing ever dies.' It is important to remember this; no matter how low you may feel or how bad a situation you may go through, hope is always there and you need to hold on to that. Behind every dark cloud sits the sun, waiting to appear.

'Hope is a good thing, maybe the best of things, and no good thing ever dies.'

BODY LANGUAGE

You can make a big difference to your own confidence and to how others see you by your body language, including the way you speak, how you walk, the way you dress, how much you smile, how enthusiastic you appear and so on. Consider how you see other people and how big a difference their body language makes. Whether that's at work, in social situations, on television or simply people you see in the shopping centre. Then consider your own body language and what you could do to improve this, which will then have a positive effect on your own confidence.

Voice and the way you speak

Your voice can play an important role in your confidence and as with many factors you can make big improvements with this with some effort and practice. Assess and rate your current voice. Perhaps ask a trusted friend for their honest opinion to identify weaknesses or areas that can be improved. People with low confidence will tend to have quieter voices, often talking with their head down, and be less assertive in their speech.

So practise talking with your head up and shoulders back, projecting the voice more, and try to speak more loudly and assertively; start by looking in the mirror and practise how you speak. It may feel a little strange, but keep practising and it will start to feel more normal and will make you sound and feel more confident

Smile and be enthusiastic

Smiling can be very powerful and very positive. Everyone has a nice smile and it is certainly better than a frown. So smile more! Make a conscious effort to smile more often and to more people and you will find it becomes infectious in a very positive way. The same goes for enthusiasm; it can become infectious and you can choose to be enthusiastic. If you do things with a positive, enthusiastic attitude and with a smile then you will generate more confidence and this will be more obvious to those who see you.

The way you stand, walk, sit, hold head, etc.

If you slump, slouch, have your head down, shoulders hunched, etc., then you are not portraying confidence. You will not feel confident or self-assured and others who see you will not think you are confident. It will give a negative, uninspiring, demotivating reaction to others and make you feel the same. Yet, with a little effort you can change that instantaneously. Pull your shoulders back, lift your head, do not slump or slouch, walk tall, stand up straight and feel what a big difference that makes; a big difference to your own confidence and also how others will see and view you. Try it and keep practising.

The way you dress and look

Similarly how you look, what you wear and the way you dress can make a big difference to how you feel and what other people's attitudes are towards you. If you are scruffy, not well presented, perhaps in clothes that are not clean, with your shirt hanging out, buttons not done up, unshaven, hair a mess, etc., then it can highlight many negatives.

'You cannot plough a field by turning it over in your mind.'

The Chimp Paradox summary

A book that I would strongly recommend is *The Chimp Paradox* by Dr Steve Peters. He is best known for being the team psychiatrist for British Cycling and Team Sky, helping the likes of Sir Chris Hoy, Sir Bradley Wiggins and Victoria Pendleton. The book is described as a mind-management plan and explains the different ways the brain works, based on neuroscience principles; this in turn helps explain the different thoughts and behaviours we have. By understanding why we think and behave in certain ways it is then possible to be more in control of our thoughts and behaviours in order to reduce any anxiety and increase our confidence, happiness and success.

I will try and explain the basics of the book and hopefully this will be helpful; however, reading *The Chimp Paradox* in full is advised for a clearer insight.

In simple terms, the brain is divided into three areas that Dr Peters describes as the Computer, the Human and the Chimp, which are all very different.

Starting with the Computer, this is the part of the brain that is full of experiences and memories built up throughout your whole life and will include both good and bad experiences. Nearly every thought and subsequent action will be based in some way on your past experiences and therefore it is important to understand the significance of those experiences and that you can change how they affect you in a positive way. If you have had bad experiences in your life then the likelihood is that they will continue to have a detrimental effect on you long after the actual experience. You may not be aware of or realise the damaging effect they can have, but these 'gremlins' are likely always to be there unless you can address them by recognising them, understanding them and then getting rid of them!

Example of a gremlin

Imagine being a 10-year-old at school, when the teacher asked a question of his pupils; you put your hand up and answered in front of the class. However, you misheard the question and your answer was very wrong. But worse than that you had simply given a wrong answer was that the rest of the children started laughing out loud and even the teacher laughed at you. You felt incredibly embarrassed and upset and that feeling haunted you for ages. Ever since you have become reluctant to speak out, answer questions, put your view across, for fear of this embarrassment happening again. You continue throughout your life being very wary and reluctant to speak up and your confidence is affected as a result.

Now let's look at this rationally and see if we can get rid of this gremlin. Firstly, we all make mistakes and get things wrong. Secondly, you were only 10 years old and the children who laughed were only 10 years old – you would have probably done the same. Thirdly, you misheard the question, which wasn't your fault. Finally, it was just one incident when you were very young – you cannot let this affect you any more. Acknowledge it happened and then rationally dispose of this gremlin. That situation will not happen again, so speak up, answer questions and you will regain confidence in this area.

Hopefully you will also have had good experiences and these are likely to continue to play a positive role in your life. Of course, the more positive experiences the better and it is important to recognise these as well as recognising the negative gremlins. The positive experiences are referred to as 'Auto-Pilots' and the aim is to increase the number of these by generating new positive experiences and also changing some of the bad experiences into positive ones, which can be possible.

The Human part of the brain is the real you and when this is active and working well then we are rational, logical, calm and mature, and our thoughts and behaviours are based upon facts and our core values. This is how we would want to behave most of the time and how we would want other people to behave. The human part of the brain has developed over hundreds of thousands of years and distinguishes us from other animals. Humans need purpose and fulfilment in their lives.

The Chimp part of the brain is at the core; it is the original part of the brain that existed before the human part developed and grew through evolution. When this part of the brain is active our behaviour can be very 'un-human' and our behaviours and thoughts are very much how we might expect a chimp to be. They will be very emotive, reactionary and impulsive, the main instinct being survival, with the options of fight, flight or freeze. So in this mood with the chimp in control we could be aggressive, excitable, anxious, scared, naughty, etc. We are not rational, we don't look at the facts, we are not logical and we are not mature.

Example of chimp and human behaviour

Let's imagine that you are going to an important meeting which is taking place at 2pm, and it is normally a thirty-minute drive or less to get to the location of the meeting. You decide to leave at 1.15pm to give yourself plenty of extra time to get there for 2pm. However, on the way there is some unexpected traffic, a combination of roadworks, temporary traffic lights and a broken-down car. You start to feel agitated and annoyed, especially as nobody seems to be doing any actual roadworks and you expect it was the owner's fault that their car broke down, causing the additional delay. You have given yourself some extra time, though, so you should still make the meeting on time. Once you are clear of the roadworks and traffic lights you then get stuck behind a really slow car and are not able to overtake. Your frustration builds and you become angrier and even more annoyed. You start to think you are going to be late for your important meeting.

Still stuck behind the slow car you decide to try a short cut and drive through a housing estate, but quite soon, with lots of cars parked on the road, you have to stop to let an oncoming car go by. You stop and wait and let the car go by, but they do not wave to say thank you or acknowledge you in any way and you are outraged. You get so angry that you are fit to explode. You can no longer concentrate on the meeting because you are so worked up that you are late and people are so rude, and you finally arrive still angry, upset and agitated.

It is clear that you have been in chimp behaviour mode! As a result of events and other people's actions out of your control you have let your chimp take over and make matters worse for you. You are upset and angry and potentially the important meeting is compromised as a result. Now if you were able to manage the chimp and have the human remain in control you would be in a much better position.

You would rationalise that you did allow plenty of extra time to get to the meeting and what happened was out of your control and you are not to blame. You would rationalise that there are always 'idiot' or 'rude' drivers out there but you cannot do anything about that. You would rationalise that the best thing for you would be to stay calm, not get upset, let it go, reassure yourself that it's not the end of the world and gain some perspective on the situation. You would apologise for being a few minutes late and explain the new traffic lights and roadworks and remain in the right mood and frame of mind for the important meeting.

The human remains rational, calm, and logical whilst the chimp gets agitated, angry, upset, emotional and reactive. In this situation it is clear that it is better for you if the human is in control and the chimp is managed.

The important initial step is to recognise when you are thinking and behaving in chimp mode. If you ask yourself the question or reflect on the situation it will be fairly obvious whether you are in human or chimp mode. If you then recognise you are indeed in the latter then you have to work out how best to manage this and how the human can regain control. If the chimp's behaviour and thinking is around anger and aggression then it may be best to allow the chimp to have a short outburst but then quickly put him away in a cage to calm down. If the behaviour and thinking is more about being worried, anxious and scared then it may be best to reassure your chimp, give him or her a hug, providing protection and security.

Part 2

Building Confidence

'Men often become what they believe themselves to be. If I believe I cannot do something, it makes me incapable of doing it. When I believe I can, I acquire the ability to do it even if I didn't have it in the beginning.' – Mahatma Gandhi

Embracing change

I am assuming the main reason that you are reading this book is to increase your own confidence, so now that, hopefully, you have a better understanding of confidence and all the contributing factors involved we can look to start building your own confidence. There are some quick wins and just having a bit more knowledge and understanding will help a little. However, to really build your confidence and to sustain a higher level going forward it will take time, effort and practice!

As with most things the more you practise the better you get, and the more time and effort you invest the better the rewards. You can increase your confidence and as a result be happier in life. Remember all the positive reasons why you want to be more confident and the effort you put in will be rewarded and will work.

Some areas will be more important than others for different people. Some areas will be more difficult, both practically and emotionally, but often the hardest things will bring the greater benefits.

And when you feel yourself becoming more confident do not stop what you have been doing! Keep doing it, keep understanding, keep learning and, of course, keep practising.

You should also be aware that certain events and experiences you will face in life will naturally lower your confidence for a period of time. It is normal and expected to have your confidence affected if, for example, you have a relationship break-up, or a bereavement, or suffer an accident, or lose your job, or anything that is a real setback and bad experience to go through.

You should expect and be prepared for a period of time when your confidence is lowered as a natural response to the event. Perhaps there is a grieving period required or a need to take some time out for yourself. Your confidence levels should return to normal fairly soon, once you have gone through the natural process of the disappointment, hurt, pain, grief, etc. Do not think your confidence is affected in the long term and do not dwell on this too much otherwise your confidence may be affected more than necessary. Accept that these things happen in life, be patient and focus on all the things that will help you and be good for you. Remember it is natural and normal to lose some confidence in these situations, no matter who you are.

Of course, when you experience some good news and some really positive experiences, enjoy and embrace them. Use that extra confidence and that wonderful feel-good factor to gain more momentum so you can further improve your confidence levels. Take the opportunity to try some new things and step out of your comfort zone so you can build stronger foundations to support and maintain your overall confidence.

Working on the 8 factors

Hopefully you have realised that there are many factors that influence and affect your confidence and that it is possible to increase your confidence with improved understanding and awareness of these. With regard to the main 8 factors, it is important to consider all of them and work out for you which areas are most relevant. Everyone will be different to some extent so really focus on those areas where you can get the best results for you.

A good exercise to do is to go through each of the eight factors in turn and write down as many current 'positives' as possible. What are the good things and what do you do well? It may be beneficial to ask someone close to you who knows you well and whose opinion you trust. What do they think about you and the positives related to each area? Spend

Positive areas	The 8 Factors	Negative areas
	YOU	
	OTHERS	
	FEARS/WORRIES	
	ACHIEVEMENT	
	SELF-IMAGE	
	SECURITY	
	HOPE/OPTIMISM	
	BODY LANGUAGE	

time on this and you may want to come back to each area two or three times to ensure you don't miss anything out.

You should also do the same exercise but with all the negatives and weakness that you feel or perceive. This can be hard and potentially upsetting but it is important in order to improve on these and increase your confidence. Highlight all the areas that you wish to improve, all the areas that concern you and cause negative thoughts, feelings and behaviours.

With a detailed list of all the positives and strengths you can then look to develop and build on these further; do not forget or underestimate all the good things. Recognise and acknowledge the positives, and get used to them, because there will be more as you build on other areas.

With the list of negatives, firstly consider how genuine and real they actually are. If you are lacking confidence it is easy to perceive things to be worse than they are or to exaggerate how bad things are. Then try to prioritise the negatives to identify those areas that are most obvious and cause the most issues in your thinking and behaviour.

'Action is a great restorer and builder of confidence.'

Practical tips, techniques and tools

As we have seen there are many factors that need to be understood and worked on so that our confidence levels can be increased and this improvement sustained for the long term. Many areas need a lot of work and time to improve whilst there are also many quick wins to be had.

In this section we look at a range of practical tips, techniques and tools that you can use both as quick wins and some, if they are practised a lot, as long-term benefits for sustained improvement. As I keep saying, everyone is different, so some of these will work better than others for different people and some will be easier than others, but give them a go and also think about creating your own techniques or adapting some of these so that they work for you.

Listen to your own advice

If a close friend told you they were lacking confidence or were worried about certain issues or a particular situation what would be your advice to them? How would you help them boost their confidence or face up to the issue and overcome it? What factors would you consider and how would you advise them in the best way?

Now consider that the close friend needing the help is actually you. Listen to your own advice and act upon it. It is very likely that you will offer great advice that will definitely help.

'Nobody can give you wiser advice than yourself' – Cicero

Avoid perfectionism

Many people have unrealistic expectations of themselves and when these are not met they beat themselves up about it, which causes a mix of problems. Nobody is perfect and nobody can be perfect. There is nothing wrong with trying your best, in fact, trying your best is fantastic and should be encouraged, but there is usually a big difference between what someone sees as perfect and what is achievable when doing your best.

Your confidence will be damaged, you will be unhappy and disappointed and you will cause yourself stress if you always expect perfection in what you do. Endeavour to do your best but recognise this is not about being perfect. Stop beating yourself up and being super-critical if you are not perfect.

Find a passion

If you are passionate about something then you are much more likely to be energised, enthusiastic, committed and motivated, which is more likely to make you feel more confident and provide enjoyment and increased happiness. What things get you excited and motivated? What are you interested in and what do you look forward to?

There is such a wide range of possibilities with finding a passion, so take time to think high and wide with options. It could be anything from cooking to climbing, ballroom dancing to bell-ringing, photography to paintballing or singing to saving endangered animals. You will be more likely to work hard, make the effort, be good at it, be successful and enjoy the experience if you find a passion or passions.

> *'Never underestimate the power of passion'* – Eve Sawyer

Stop trying to please everyone

A common problem we have is trying to please other people all the time and often we find the more we lack confidence the more we focus on trying to please others rather than focusing on ourselves. You can never please everyone. So you will always fail if you try to do this. It is your life and you are the most important person to try and please, and when you feel good you will automatically benefit those people in your life that you care about. Be kind to yourself.

Worry less about what others think, stop trying to seek approval or recognition from people, live your life according to your values and focus on what is best for you rather than trying to please everyone else all the time. It will take effort and practice but you can do this.

> *'If we want to feel truly confident, we must break the habit of trying to please all people, all of the time'* – Gael Lindenfield

Don't avoid

If you find yourself avoiding things, people and situations and have become more withdrawn and reclusive you need to work on this to make sure it doesn't get worse. Sometimes it is advisable and beneficial to avoid certain situations, but the danger is that you can soon end up losing important social skills and becoming more distant from people and places, restricting your opportunities to enjoy life and have more positive experiences.

Build up slowly if you have found yourself in this position. At first you may look to get outside your house and go for a walk on your own for a short while. Next time you may make the effort to say 'hello' to someone you pass on your walk. You may then go to a busier area like a shopping centre where there are many people about but you don't have to engage with them. The next step may be to have a short conversation with a cashier or assistant at a shop by asking them a question or wishing them a pleasant day. Gradually you are building up your contact with other people step by step and gaining confidence in those situations. You may try to meet up with a friend for a coffee and chat and look to make more conversations with people, whether that's at work, at the shops or with other friends. Over time you will develop improved social skills and the confidence so that you are more comfortable and at ease in those situations.

Finger/thumb

If you are in a situation where you feel you need an instant boost of confidence, for example, about to do a presentation, go for a job interview, go on a first date, about to start a race, or halfway through an exam, then this technique can be quite effective. Firstly think about someone you admire and respect, perhaps a hero or mentor. It could be someone you know personally or someone you haven't met but is a huge inspiration to you. Think about this person and all the positives and reasons why you have chosen them.

Then if you are ever in need of a confidence boost, rather than crossing your fingers and just hoping, you can squeeze your finger and thumb together and think about this person. Think about their qualities, why they are an inspiration and what they would do in this situation. Let their inspiration boost your confidence. Try it!

5 regrets on your deathbed

I don't know if this is actually true, but in a way it doesn't matter because the sentiment and message is very clear. A survey was carried out in Australia by a nurse at a hospital treating terminally ill patients, and the top five regrets of those people dying were as follows:

- *I wish I'd had the courage to live a life true to myself, not the life others expected of me.*
- *I wish I hadn't worked so hard.*
- *I wish I'd had the courage to express my feelings.*
- *I wish I had stayed in touch with my friends.*
- *I wish that I had let myself be happier.*

Take some time to think about this. What can you visualise yourself saying if you were in that same position? Be honest and reflective and write down your own list. What does that tell you? Remember, you only get one life but you get lots of opportunities. Make the most of those opportunities.

Step out of your comfort zone

A great way of boosting confidence is to try something out of your comfort zone. Doing something that you wouldn't normally do in a positive way, achieving something that you didn't think you could achieve or having an experience you've never encountered before can be wonderful for your confidence.

In my experience and from listening and observing other people, it is clear that in the majority of cases where people have stepped out of their comfort zone and done something they have been pleased with the results, often ecstatic and have certainly not regretted it. It can not only boost confidence but it can open doors up to other opportunities that can lead to more positive outcomes and experiences. Even if things don't work out then you can be proud of the fact that you tried something out of your comfort zone, and you can learn from the experience. So go for it, take a few risks and step out of your normal comfort zone.

'Take risks: if you win, you will be happy; if you lose, you will be wise.'

Positive past memories

It is very likely that you have some positive memories from the past that can provide a confidence boost to you. Think about situations, events or experiences that you have had that have been really positive on a personal level. Recall the feeling, the pride, the passion, the success, the achievement and use it to inspire, motivate and boost your confidence in the present moment.

For example, I have completed several marathons and on each one I can remember crossing the finishing line with the crowds cheering and the mix of positive emotions, the feeling of relief yet elation,the personal achievement and pride making the pain and sacrifice worth it, and the confidence gained from doing that and thinking if I can do this then I can do anything! If I need a confidence boost, or some extra motivation while training then I have a bank of these experiences that I can use to help. Create your own bank of positive memories and call upon them when you need to.

Find a mentor

If you are lucky enough to have a good mentor in your life then you will know how beneficial they can be. A good mentor is a person you can talk to, seek advice from, discuss issues with and whom you trust and who has your best interests at heart; someone who has experience, knowledge and wisdom that can be passed on to you in order to help you develop as a person, which in turn adds to your confidence.

If you don't have a mentor, then why not see if you can find one. Make some efforts to identify a person you respect and trust who can offer some of their time and experiences in a way that will be beneficial for you. Perhaps it could be someone at work, possibly a family member or friend of a friend. If you believe they could be a good mentor then ask them if they would consider filling that role. It may not work out, but if you don't try you won't know and if it does work then the added value and benefits will be worth it.

Music

Listening to your favourite music, especially upbeat and positive tracks, can really lift your mood, it can release some adrenaline, increase your energy and boost your confidence. Whether it's before you go out, ahead of a meeting, in the build-up to a race or challenge, prior to a presentation you are delivering or just for more general situations, it is definitely worth trying.

Music is usually readily available at home, in the car, on your computer or phone etc., so take advantage and try it. Play music that you associate with happy memories – a holiday, a party, an event when you were relaxed and confident, enjoying your life heartily. And as long as it is appropriate then why not try singing aloud or dancing around to the music too!

Act like a confident person

Many people who appear confident are in fact acting. They are able to put on a front when needed and act like a confident person. With a little bit of practice you can also do this and as a result your confidence is likely to improve as a result of acting like a confident person.

Imagine how you would think, act and behave if you were a confident person and then look to replicate that for real and become an actor. You may find it easier to act in this way in an environment away from your normal situation. So perhaps if you go away for a weekend, or visit a new town or shopping centre or when you meet a new group of people, then this can be your opportunity to practice acting like a confident person. It may feel strange but there is a good chance that you can pull it off and you feel more comfortable acting this way, and it becomes more normal the more you practise. Going forward you may also find the gap between acting like a confident person and actually being a confident person becomes smaller and smaller.

Never be jealous

Jealousy is one of the most negative, unproductive and destructive emotions there is. Nothing good can come of being jealous and the sooner you realise, accept this and strip away any jealous thoughts and behaviours from your life the better your life will be.

Thinking about someone else's situation with envy and being jealous of what they have or what they are doing will eat away at you in a very negative way. A jealous person is not a nice person and jealousy will never lead to anything positive or beneficial for that person. Jealousy uses a lot of energy and can be consuming and, most importantly, it affects only you – not the person you envy. Therefore, it's a complete waste of time, energy and wayward thought processes.

The best advice is whenever you start to get a jealous thought, recognise it and then say no and chuck it out of your head. Do not entertain those thoughts for any time at all. Keep practising and it will become easier to chuck away those thoughts. A life without jealousy is a much happier, content and confident life than one where jealousy exists.

Handle criticism

It is likely that there will be times throughout your life when you will be criticised for something. On occasions this will be justified and on others it will be unfair and unjustified. However, your ability to handle criticism is very important. If it is justified then the ability to take on board the criticism and look to make positive changes to improve is necessary. Do not become defensive and closed to constructive feedback and criticism. Understand, accept and then look to improve. Too often people become very defensive and take criticism very badly and when it is justified it means they will continue making the same mistakes.

Also, it is important to be able to handle criticism when it is unfair and not justified. Being able to ignore it, forget it, let it go and move on without it affecting you adversely. This can be difficult, but unless you develop tools and techniques to ignore the unfair and unjust criticism it can eat away at you and cause problems, especially regarding your confidence. Everyone has a right to an opinion but that doesn't mean it is right. Often the unfair criticism will not be based on facts or take into account all the factors, or the critic's knowledge will be limited or they have their own personal issues going on which distorts their view. So take this into account and if you feel this is the case then let it go and move on.

Give compliments

It is nice to receive compliments from people and this can often help improve your confidence. However, it is also nice to give compliments and this too can enhance your own confidence and self-esteem. You will usually find that the more confident a person is then the more likely they are to give other people compliments. So start practising complimenting people and see what happens.

I don't advise just handing out compliments for the sake of it but when the situation arises where there is an opportunity to give a genuine compliment to someone then try it. It could be a friend, a family member, a work colleague or even a complete stranger. Tell them you like their hair or their coat, let them know they have a wonderful smile or you admire their tenacity, perhaps they make you laugh or you find them really interesting. Whatever the potential compliment, think about saying it and then do it in a nice, polite and genuine way; it will not only be nice for them to receive but you will feel better too and it can help improve your mood and confidence levels.

Learn to say no

Many people find it is very difficult to say no to other people and often as a result they get taken advantage of, which is not in their best interests and usually decreases their confidence further. They become a soft touch and end up doing things they don't want to do and become frustrated and upset as a result. They can't seem to end the cycle, as the more they say yes the more it happens and the lower their confidence becomes.

The ability to say no can be really important. Being able to stand up for yourself, being more assertive and saying no when you believe that saying no is the right thing to do are characteristics of a confident person. So if you are lacking confidence it is harder to do and compounds the problem. But once you learn to say no it becomes easier. You gain confidence and feel more comfortable in standing up for yourself and being more assertive. Try it, practise it and you will feel much better as a result.

Nervous face

Here is a quick exercise that can be fun and also very effective in combating nerves. Stand in front of a mirror and pull a 'happy/smiley/joyful' face. Next pull a 'sad/upset/miserable' face. Next pull a 'shocked/surprised' face. Finally pull a 'nervous' face.

What did you notice? Hopefully you will realise that it is usually very obvious what the emotion is, whether that's happy, sad or shocked, due to the facial expressions that the person shows. But when it comes to being nervous there is literally no emotion. It is a blank, still, emotionless expression that comes across. There is nothing in your face that shows or expresses your nerves and anxiety.

So when you are in that situation where you are nervous and anxious and you are worried that everyone will know how nervous you are then just remember they cannot tell from your facial expression. There is no expression of nerves, therefore they will not know, and you can be reassured that people won't be thinking how nervous you are.

Let things go

There will always be experiences and events in your life that will cause upset and pain, or people who hurt you and let you down. All too often these difficult and damaging experiences continue to affect us negatively long after the actual event has happened. For your health, happiness and confidence it is important as much as possible to move on from these. If you can look to forgive and forget and learn to let things go then it is likely to be in your interests.

It can be hard to understand why certain things have happened and often you will not find the answers you want. This can eat away at you, whether you are aware or not, and the more you focus on past episodes and people that create negative and harmful feelings for you the longer the damage lasts. It is difficult to move forward in a positive way if you carry the negative shackles and chains of past experiences. Sometimes you just have to accept that you won't get an answer, you may never understand, things happen, people do stuff and the best thing for you is to let things go and move on with your life.

> *'You can't have a better tomorrow if you are thinking about yesterday all the time.'* – *Charles F Kettering*

Quotes

Reading a quote can be so simple, yet effective in providing hope, motivation, inspiration, perspective and guidance. Here are a few that seem relevant, but there are thousands of great quotes out there so go and find your favourites or make up some of your own.

- *The older I get, the less I care about what people think of me. Therefore the older I get, the more I enjoy life.*

- *Ask yourself this question: Will this matter a year from now?*

- *Everything in life is temporary. So if things are going good, enjoy it because it won't last forever. And if things are going bad, don't worry it can't last forever either.*

- *If it is important to you, you will find a way. If not you'll find an excuse.*

- *It's better to walk alone, than with a crowd going in the wrong direction.*

- *Don't let what you can't do stop you from doing what you can do.*

- *He who fears being conquered is sure of defeat.*

- *A pessimist sees the difficulty in every opportunity, an optimist sees the opportunity in every difficulty.*

- *Courage is the discovery that you may not win, and trying when you know you can lose.*

- *Real difficulties can be overcome; it is only the imaginary ones that are unconquerable.*

- *We must not let our fears hold us back from pursuing our hopes.*

Inspiring stories

You can gain a lot of confidence, hope and inspiration from other people and their stories. There are so many examples of inspiration, triumph over adversity, the will to succeed, belief in dreams, etc., which can be used to motivate you and in turn help build your confidence. Here is a great example of a real-life inspirational story.

Dick Fosbury was an American high jumper who changed his sport forever by adopting, at the time, a completely new technique to high jumping which became known as the 'Fosbury Flop'. For the last few decades every single one of the world's top high jumpers has used the technique he created, but in 1968 at the Mexico Olympics he was the only person who did. He was a relatively unknown athlete who came away with an Olympic gold medal and new Olympic high jump record.

He always enjoyed sport and was a reasonable athlete during school, competing in a few high jump competitions at local school level without huge success. Back in the 1960s there were two main techniques that high jumpers used – the straddle and the scissors technique. With the straddle you effectively threw yourself over the bar head first on your front. With the scissors you went over the bar in an upright seated position. Dick Fosbury's athletics coach tried to encourage the straddle technique, whilst Dick Fosbury himself preferred the scissors technique, yet with both of these he was well below the standards of a state champion, let alone a national champion.

Fosbury then started to play about with his technique and found that if he went over the bar leaning backwards, in a scissor-kick style but then flipping his backside over the bar he was able to clear heights he had not previously been able to. Despite his coach being dismissive of this new technique and trying to encourage him to work on the straddle, Dick Fosbury persevered with his own technique and his confidence and belief in this grew.

His personal best kept improving and people started to take notice, yet at the same time people and spectators were laughing at this strange new way of high jumping. A newspaper termed it the 'Fosbury Flop' and the name stuck. He continued to make huge improvements and simply ignored all the people who rubbished him or laughed at him, and in 1968 he qualified as one of three members of the USA team for the Mexico Olympics. He was still a relatively unknown athlete and was seen more as a circus act than a gold medal prospect. He won the event and became Olympic champion. People took notice and jumpers took notice. He changed history and within a few Olympic Games every high jumper had adopted his technique.

He found his own way and methods, grew in confidence and stuck to his beliefs. His confidence grew because he was getting results and he knew it was working. So find what works for you and if you are getting results keep going. Have the confidence to keep going with what you believe in if it works for you.

People

As previously discussed, the people around you can have a big impact on your confidence both positively and negatively. So if you have people you know that impact you positively then try to meet them, spend time with them, talk with them and let their qualities help you to increase your confidence. They will want to help and you may decide to tell them the positive effect they have. What a great compliment to receive from someone! You may need to make an effort, take a bit of extra time out or travel to see them but it will be worth it in order to feel better and get that confidence boost.

Also, you can ask friends what they most like about you and what they think your best qualities are. You can let them know that you are feeling a bit low in confidence and the responses they give will almost certainly remind you of some of your great qualities. Listen to the compliments, accept them, and most importantly, never ignore them, and use them to have a more positive and confident outlook.

> *'Be who you are and say what you feel, because those who mind don't matter, and those who matter don't mind.'* – Dr Seuss

Visualise

A well-known and often effective technique that can be used is to visualise what you want actually happening. The more you visualise it the more likely it is to happen. With visualisation usually comes focus and if it is a positive focus you are also more likely to believe it will happen and be more confident the outcome will be the one you want.

It could be visualising a job interview going well, so rather than worrying about saying something wrong or not coming across well, you are instead visualising a great interview, focusing on the positives. It could be during a running race you are finding things tough but you start to visualise yourself crossing the finish line, succeeding in your goals, feeling the sense of achievement and pride and how positive that is. It could be attending a new group event and visualising lots of nice, friendly, welcoming people and feeling comfortable and enjoying the occasion.

By visualising particular situations in a positive way with positive outcomes you are being productive and it will help give you the confidence to go ahead with that situation rather than worrying about it.

Makeover

Take some time to give yourself a treat of a makeover. Perhaps it could be a new haircut or style, buy some new clothes, go for a facial or other beauty treatment or you could buy a new perfume or aftershave to wear. Make some effort and invest some time and money (appropriately) for yourself.

If you take that time and make that investment you will feel better about how you look and feel as well as how you come across to others, which will naturally boost your confidence. Other people are also likely to notice and you may get some additional compliments and positive feedback as a bonus, although what you think and how you feel is the most important thing.

Jokes, facts, stories

You will all know people who always seem to have something interesting to say, stories to tell, facts they can recall and jokes they share. They generally come across as interesting, funny, intelligent and confident. Wouldn't it be good to have these skills and be able to do similarly if the opportunity arises? How great would it feel if you could do this and people thought you were all those things? You would undoubtedly feel more confident.

Well, there is no reason why you can't improve on this by learning some jokes, reading more books, learning more facts, watching more news and current affairs, thinking about some great stories and examples from your own life. It may help to write them down, think about them more, practise telling them, etc., so that if and when the opportunity arises you feel more comfortable sharing these stories, facts and jokes. Step by step you will feel more confident and comfortable in group conversations and by participating you won't feel left out, you won't be sat wishing you could join in and feeling negative about that. With some effort you can really build your confidence in this way.

Learn to laugh at yourself

Do you take yourself too seriously? When you do something wrong or stupid or make a mistake do you beat yourself up about it? Are you particularly hard on yourself and not give yourself a break especially when things don't go as you would like them to? Do you ever smile and laugh at yourself when you do sometimes make a mistake?

We all make mistakes; we all do stupid things at times or get things wrong. Sometimes it is best just to laugh at yourself. Understand that you are not perfect and it is OK to do something stupid occasionally. When something goes wrong try laughing at the situation rather than beating yourself up and getting upset or angry. It won't always work but at times the best thing to do is just laugh at yourself and not take things quite so seriously. Your confidence will be dented if you always blame yourself, get upset, beat yourself up or get angry at mistakes you make. So practise smiling and laughing at yourself more and it might just be a good thing.

> *'If at first you don't succeed, try, try again. Then quit. There's no use being a damn fool about it.'* – W.C Fields

Good luck charm or action

Some people find that having a lucky charm with them can boost their confidence in certain situations or provide a little bit of extra security which will help them. Perhaps something they carry with them on their key ring or in their handbag or wear on their wrist. Anything that the owner feels is lucky for them and can give them that little something extra when needed could be very beneficial.

Alternatively it could be an action you carry out to give you luck or a superstitious behaviour that you believe could help. The obvious action is to cross your fingers but you may have any kind of action or act that works for you. It could work and you have nothing to lose so why not try something out?

New skills

Are you impressed if someone has a skill or a natural aptitude for something? Do you have more respect for them? Do you see them in a more positive light? There are so many skills that you could learn that will help build confidence. Examples could include learning a foreign language, painting, photography, writing, juggling, martial arts, cooking and the list could go on and on. It could be a new skill that is relevant to your career or simply a new hobby. But learning a new skill will have many benefits and is very likely to help increase your confidence, so think about things you may wish to do and look at how you could go about learning these new skills.

By learning a new skill, the chances are that you may have contact with others who have the same goals and this will enable you to interact with like-minded people. Immediately you have met others on common ground and this will enable you to be more relaxed and confident.

Hug the chimp

As discussed in the section on the Chimp Paradox, it is important to understand and manage your own chimp. There are various ways to do this but one of the most effective is simply to reassure your chimp and give it a hug! A hug from anyone can be very powerful but with your own chimp it is usually about providing reassurance, security, showing you care and understand and being there in a positive way. If the chimp is scared, anxious, worried, concerned and upset then the best thing to do is usually to give it a big hug and let it know you are there and things will be OK.

Exercises to try

Walk tall

Practice walking tall with your shoulders back and head held high. Try walking a little more quickly than usual and with more purpose. You may want to practise this at home first or find a place where there is no one else about. How does it feel? Do you notice a difference?

As you practise this more try doing it as part of your normal routine, whether that's walking to work, around the office, in the shopping centre, etc. You should notice that by walking more confidently you start to feel more confident and it becomes more natural.

Affirmations

Write down a list of all your strengths, good points, successes and achievements. Take your time with this and once you have a list go and stand in front of a mirror and read it out loud.

Make sure you look at yourself when you say the words and speak clearly and loudly (you may want to make sure you are alone or put on some music!). Keep repeating this and speak the words with more conviction and more confidence. Recognise your strengths and achievements, praise yourself and remind yourself that you have done these things and have these qualities and strengths that are a real positive.

Chatting to strangers

How great would it feel to be comfortable chatting to and holding a conversation with anyone, whether you know them as friends or acquaintances or they are complete strangers? Try starting off with the more straightforward 'hello, thank you, have a nice day, how are you?' etc. Make sure you smile and make eye contact, too.

Good people to try this with are shop assistants, cashiers, store managers and security people you see in everyday circumstances. The more you try, the easier it becomes and you can start trying to add in more conversation like 'have you got any plans for the weekend?', 'I can't believe how bad the weather is', 'do you live in the area?', 'where is your accent from?', 'I like your hair', etc. Keep trying new things and it will become more comfortable and your confidence will grow.

Recall your chimp behaviour

Having read about the differences in your 'human' and 'chimp' behaviour and thoughts, try writing down examples of your own chimp behaviour during a particular day. Document the different occasions where you got angry, upset, anxious, reacted to something, got excitable, lost your temper, jumped to conclusions, etc.

By reflecting on your behaviour and thoughts and recognising the differences between human and chimp you will be in a better position to manage the chimp. The more you recognise and become aware of it, the easier it will be to take control and manage the situation. Also, you can try reflecting on other people's behaviour and actions and notice when they are likely to have been in chimp mode!

Super-confident powers

Take a bit of time to think what you would do if you were made super-confident by wearing a super-confident powers cloak! Imagine if you had no confidence issues at all and believed you could pretty much do and succeed in anything with your super-confident powers. Write down the things you would do and would like to achieve and imagine yourself with these special new powers. How does it feel?

The more you imagine you have the super powers and visualise the things you would do and how it would feel then the more chance that this could happen. With more effort and practice it can be possible, and having that possibility will hopefully keep you motivated to keep understanding and building your confidence and to keep practising the techniques and doing those things that work for you.

Empathise

Take time to try and understand why people say what they say and do what they do and behave how they behave. The more empathy you can demonstrate, the easier it is to understand people's behaviour and actions. And the more you understand, the better placed you are not to let negative experiences and people affect you.

For example, if someone does or says something to you that upsets you or knocks your confidence, but actually there is a reason, because their own issues have led them to behave in that way. Without empathy and understanding of the other person this could knock you back, but by realising they don't mean it and it's a reflection on them rather than you then you will not feel knocked or affected negatively. Empathy is a great skill to have and can be improved with practice and more time spent working on it.

Energise yourself

Often you will be feeling lethargic and this lack of energy will do nothing for your confidence, so try an exercise to energise yourself, get the blood flowing and feel more alive. If you feel more energised then this will only help you with your confidence in a variety of situations.

You may have to modify or adapt your energising technique depending on your location or situation, but something like waving your arms about for ten seconds, clapping your hands, jogging on the spot, doing a few star jumps, spinning round in circles, a couple of press-ups or some shadow boxing could all help. Try it and get that blood pumping and energy increased.

Make your confidence cocktail

If you imagine all the different ingredients that can be used in making different drink cocktails then it is similar to all the factors that can go into making a confident person. So write down all the good, positive strengths and attributes you have. Include successes, achievements, good people in your life, great experiences you've had and other qualities you have.

Then when you feel like you need a confidence boost try making some cocktails using all those ingredients and factors. Experiment with different ingredients and work out what you like best, what tastes good and how easily it can be made. Visualise making your own range of cocktails and when you need one then grab the ingredients, give it a shake and pour yourself a drink.

Practise, practise, practise

There are many 'quick wins' to increasing your confidence; however, some of these will not last unless you keep doing them. More importantly, if you really want to increase your confidence for the long term and be 'good at being confident' then it really is a case of practise, practise, practise! As the saying goes, 'the more you practise the better you get', and this is very true with building confidence.

Let's look at an analogy to highlight the point. If you had low confidence and wanted to be much more confident you could relate this to being a slow, unfit runner who wishes to be able to run a marathon. You are capable of running a marathon but not straight away. It will take several months to build up the strength, the fitness, the stamina, the belief, etc. and the same applies to confidence. You need to practise over time and slowly but surely you will achieve the goal.

You will also need to look at many factors. With running a marathon you will be look-ing at other factors than just running such as footwear, other clothing, your nutrition, hydration, other types of training, training partners, motivation, advice, encouragement and much more. In order to go from being a poor runner to being a good runner there are many elements to work on, many factors to consider and it will take time and a lot of practice.... otherwise you won't be able to do it.

With building confidence you need to look at all the factors, build it up over time and keep practising. You will undoubtedly have some dips along the journey but as long as you are sensible, realistic and keep practising then you will succeed. You will build up confidence and the rewards will be worth the effort.

It could help to write a list of things you feel should do to benefit you and build your confidence based upon what you have already considered and understood so far. Make sure they fit with your personal strengths, weaknesses, positives and negatives that you have identified. The list should be comprehensive with a mix of the quick wins, practical tips, and longer-term aims, and if you think of more things then keep adding to your list.

As long as you are being productive and positive towards building your confidence you will achieve results. The more you practise the easier it will become and the better you will get. Seek advice, support and encouragement from others when needed, but remember that ultimately this is your responsibility and you need to be the one to make the effort, make the changes and put in the practice.

If we go back to the running a marathon analogy, it is very likely that along the journey of going from being a novice runner to being able to complete a marathon you will have some setbacks. Perhaps an injury, a couple of bad training days, an illness that prevents you running or a lack of belief that you can do it. The same is likely to happen as you go along your journey of building your confidence, but you need to keep patient and keep believing and you will keep moving forward. Don't let the setbacks deter you from your goal.

> *'People tell me I'm lucky, but I've noticed the harder I practise, the luckier I get.'*
> *– Gary Player*

Real-life examples

In this section we look at a few of the more common examples of real-life situations where people often struggle with regard to their confidence. From the questionnaires previously mentioned, the workshops and chatting to people, I find the examples below often feature when people are asked about difficult situations and how their confidence is a factor.

Asking someone out

Imagine you are single and there is someone you like and you would love to find out more about them and get to know them better. So the plan is to speak to them and ask them out for a drink or a meal. However, the idea of approaching them and asking them out fills you with dread. What do I say to them? What if they say no and reject me? What if they feel insulted I asked them out? What if they laugh at me? All these negative thoughts and outcomes occupy your mind and the more you think about it the more frustrated you get with yourself and the more apprehensive you become. Perhaps it is best not to say anything to avoid any embarrassment and rejection?

You need to look at this from the positive angle. What if she says yes and you go out and you have a great time and it's the beginning of a wonderful relationship? OK, she may say no because she is already seeing someone, but she says she is flattered and is really pleasant about it. You feel good because you had the courage to ask her out and although she said no it was all done in a nice way and gives you the confidence to ask someone else out in the future. OK, she says no and isn't very nice about it. You feel a bit despondent and disappointed but actually her reaction showed a not very attractive side to her and your view of her has diminished, so actually you are not too fussed about it after all.

So in a way you can't really lose! Be pleasant, be polite, smile, focus on the potential positive outcomes and go for it. Life is too short to have those 'what ifs', so take a chance and in nearly all cases it will be OK and work out. As the saying goes 'If you don't ask you don't get.'

Job interviews

For many people job interviews present a huge barrier and they can cause a lot of worry, stress and anxiety. A lack of confidence will affect the person in the build-up to the interview as well as during the interview, which could affect their chances of success. You could be looking to progress your career or perhaps you are currently unemployed and are looking for the role that can get you back into work or a new career.

Preparation is key to job interviews. Do your homework and find out about the role, the company and the person interviewing you, if possible. Know your CV inside out, think about the likely questions they will ask and have answers prepared. Also think of relevant questions you can ask the interviewer. Take time to prepare and do your homework.

Now try to visualise the interview in a calm, rational and positive way. Whenever a negative thought pops into your head, stop and erase it and then continue in a positive way. You are polite, enthusiastic, positive, calm and confident that you are right for this job. You want to enjoy the interview and you want it to be a pleasant experience for the interviewer too. If you are overly nervous, worried or agitated it could make the interviewer feel uncomfortable, so visualise a formal but friendly conversation.

As long as you have prepared well there is not much else you can do other than try to keep relaxed, be enthusiastic and be friendly and polite. You can do that! Preparation builds the confidence and keeping a positive mindset creates the enthusiasm, and being a nice person will make you friendly and polite. If you can, see if you can practise a mock interview with a friend, especially if you know someone who has carried out job interviews themselves.

Try to enjoy the experience and don't dwell on anything you feel you did or said during the interview. And use the finger/thumb technique, the super-confident powers cloak or act as a confident person to give you that boost if needed.

Going on a date

You are looking for a relationship and you have arranged a date but you are really nervous about the occasion. What will you wear, what will they be like, will they like you, will you say or do something stupid, will you like them, will they find you interesting or funny, etc.?

The likelihood is that the other person will be going through similar emotions and have the same thoughts. You are best trying to make them feel as comfortable and relaxed as possible and that starts with being polite, friendly and nice, and make sure you smile! A smile is one of the most effective ways of making people feel at ease.

Think about some questions you could ask about the other person and be prepared to listen. Listening and allowing the other person to chat is very important. Give compliments too and don't be afraid to laugh at yourself if you do say or do anything stupid. Relax and enjoy the experience as two adults enjoying some company.

Try to be yourself as much as possible with what you say, what you wear, how you act, etc. and if you have a good time with the person then great; let them know. If it doesn't work out then don't worry about it, there are many other people out there and it is better to be patient and find someone right for you rather than worrying about someone who isn't.

Public speaking

For many people the fear of public speaking ranks very high on the most-feared list; standing up in front of a group or crowd of people with all eyes and ears focused on what you say, how you say it, what you do and how you do it. Perhaps it is a presentation you have to do at work or for a local group of which you are a member. It could be you are doing a best man's speech at a wedding or have been asked to say some words at a funeral. There are many examples of situations that could be described as public speaking and there are a lot of fears attached to this for a lot of people.

One of the best ways to get over these fears and perform well without a huge amount of anxiety is to be passionate and knowledgeable about the subjects you are covering. Being passionate is a great way to feel more confident and remove fears, and knowledge is similar. So the more passionate and knowledgeable you are the easier it will be, so make sure you know the subject matter.

Other techniques that will also help include visualising the event and to practising your speech or presentation, putting on your super-confident powers cloak and remembering that nobody wants you to mess up. People will want you to speak well and will be supportive, so stop thinking of anything negative and instead focus on the content and delivery of the talk in a relaxed, controlled way. And as with a job interview, try to enjoy the experience.

Running a marathon

Let's imagine that you would like to run a marathon one day; perhaps it's on your bucket list or you've been inspired by someone or by watching the London Marathon on the TV. However, although you have run more than a few miles previously, you don't consider yourself a good runner and the thought of running so far and for so long scares you. You currently have no confidence that you could achieve that goal and although you want to do it, you don't think it is realistic.

Firstly, you need to give yourself an appropriate time period and seek the advice appropriate for you. Although it is important to remind yourself of the long-term goal and the reasons why you wish to achieve this, the best advice to start with is to break down the distance into manageable chunks over the time period. If you give yourself 6 months to train from scratch then during that time you want to be able to run at least 20 miles before you run the marathon. If you could run 2 miles now then that is an addition of 18 miles over 6 months or 3 miles per month. Your new target becomes adding 3 miles a month. You can do that!

Of course you need to make time to fit in some runs and also other training. If you can find a training partner or group that can help, but make sure you progress at your own speed rather than feeling intimidated or out of your depth. Your confidence will build slowly and steadily, as will your physical ability, and this is better than trying to go too quickly too soon ,which is more likely to lead to injury and loss of confidence.

Other factors like running shoes, clothing, running watch, food, hydration, nutrition, sleep, etc. will also be important. But as long as you put in the effort you will progress and your confidence will build, step by step. And you might even enjoy it!

Undoubtedly you will have a few bad days and poor runs but this will always happen, so don't worry, just stick to your programme, building up your strength, fitness and confidence. Don't listen too much to other people, as this is your challenge, your run and your achievement.

So much of running is about relaxing and being able to control your breathing and conserving energy, so any worries and stresses and negative thinking affect this. Be confident that you will be OK; you have done the training, you will get the pace right and you will relax and enjoy the event.

It will be extremely tough but keep reminding yourself you can do it and will do it and when you do your confidence will rocket further. You can use that experience to do other things and further your confidence even more. The achievement was built upon preparation, planning and patience, with your physical ability increasing in line with your confidence.

Going to a social event

You've been invited to a social event, let's say a friend's evening wedding reception and you have been dreading it for weeks. You are lacking confidence and the idea of going to a large social event on your own with many people you don't know fills you with fear. You have been anxious, not sleeping well due to worry and have started thinking of excuses not to go. You have been focusing on all the negatives and worrying about what could go wrong, what people will think of you and how bad you might feel. You get annoyed with yourself for thinking like this and you wish you could go, enjoy yourself and not be so worried.

You should look at this as an opportunity to enjoy yourself, perhaps treat yourself to a makeover, a new outfit, a haircut, etc., and really focus on how good the event could be.

You will see some old friends, meet some new people, let your hair down a bit, relax and have some fun. There will be many other people there who probably are nervous too but the atmosphere will be friendly, informal and welcoming. It will be a celebration of the happy couple's day and the focus will be on them, not on your apprehension and low confidence. It gives you the chance to practise talking to strangers in a risk-free environment, as you can ask them how they know the couple, if they attended the service, where they have come from, what their job is, etc.

All the worry and focusing on the negatives will not help the situation or your confidence. Visualising a great evening, practising your confidence-boosting techniques, allowing yourself to have a good time, relaxing and treating yourself will all help you and once you are there you will enjoy it and you will wonder why you were ever so worried about it all.

Talking to your boss

For some time you have wanted to talk to your boss about a number of issues, including a few things you are not happy about and also some ideas that you think could improve the company. You have held back through fear of what they will say and how they will react. You don't want to cause problems and you are not very confident when dealing with your boss; however, you are becoming increasingly frustrated and unhappy with some of these issues and you feel you should say something.

In a situation like this you must be prepared as much as possible with facts, evidence, documentation, etc., and always look to come forward with solutions to any problems you may raise. No boss wants to hear just problems! So with regard to the issues you are not happy with make sure you have looked at all the factors, perhaps discuss them with another colleague or a friend to get a clear, unbiased view and then present the details in a calm, assured way along with specific things you would like to see done. With regard to the ideas to improve the company, make sure they are clear and concise and thought through and present them in a positive and enthusiastic way. This should be applauded as it shows initiative and is in the best interests of your company and your boss.

Think about the positives of the situation – the issues affecting you might be addressed and you could get praised for your ideas. All you can do is your best by presenting the information clearly, and in most cases this will be well received. It is far better to do this than for you not to say anything and become more unhappy, and then someone else comes up with your ideas to improve the company and they get the credit!

Climbing a mountain

Imagine you are climbing a mountain for the first time and for this example let's imagine you are taking part in one of the 'Climb Your Mountain' weekend trips. You are worried about a number of things, including will you be able to reach the top? will you hold everyone else up? do you have the right equipment? what happens if the weather is bad? what if you get injured during the climb? etc. Most of the worries and concerns are focusing on negative possibilities which are compounded by your lack of confidence generally and also specifically to climbing a mountain which you have not done before.

There are many things you can do and should remember that will help you. You will be advised on the right equipment, food, drink, clothing, etc., so as long as you listen to the right advice from the right person then you will be OK and can do no more. It is not a race, so you will be able to take your time, and pacing your efforts will be key. The mountain leader will take care of you and pace you accordingly. It is not a 'climb' – it is a walk uphill then downhill! You can walk and you should be confident in your ability to walk, it is not climbing. If anything does go wrong with the weather, injury or equipment then you will be looked after, you do not need to worry.

You have the right clothing and equipment, you are with an experienced and knowledgeable guide, you are walking rather than climbing, you can take your time as you are not racing, you will be supported, motivated and encouraged by others, you will see wonderful scenery, you will feel a great sense of pride and achievement and once completed your confidence levels will be greatly boosted and you will want to do more similar challenges. Prepare in the right way, utilise the best people, understand what you are actually doing, enjoy the experience, focus on the positives, take your time and pace yourself and you will have a great time and you will do it!

Overview and going forward

'Though no one can go back and make a brand new start, anyone can start from now and make a brand new ending.'

I hope you have found the book helpful and it has, at the very least, got you thinking about the many different factors that can influence confidence and thus provide a framework for you to increase your own confidence and indeed help others to increase theirs.

I would suggest rereading this book a few times and take the time to really understand how the different factors affect you and the areas that are most likely to help you. Jot down the points which really made an impact or highlight them and copy down some of the quotes for inspiration. Think about the reasons why you want to feel more confident and believe that with effort you will definitely increase your confidence and reap the rewards. At times it will feel tough and your motivation to keep practising might fade, but if you remind yourself of the benefits and take your time then you will succeed.

The positive thinking and positive actions will become easier and more habitual. You will learn to be less fearful and be confident that you can deal with any failures that occur. You will do more productive things, achieve more, feel more fulfilled, laugh more, smile more and feel happier. Each time you do these your confidence will increase and the foundations for this increased confidence will be strong and sustainable.

The fragile foundations you may have had before will be replaced with permanent, strong building blocks. Yes, you will have some bad days and feel negative at times and less confident, but those times will become rarer, less frequent and when they do happen you will have the confidence to know they are only temporary and know you have the tools to deal with them.

You will find it easier to rid yourself of the negative, damaging people in your life and instead attract the true friends and positive people that can make such a difference. You will be one of those trustworthy, genuine, positive and confident people that others admire and respect.

Everything will become easier and you will learn to embrace the good times and deal with the bad times. You will have the understanding, tools and techniques to face the inevitable issues and people that in the past would have caused you so much grief, worry and despair.

Your life will be fuller, richer, more productive, more positive and happier because of your increased levels of confidence and that will be due to two things – your improved understanding of all the factors and your efforts to keep practising and practising!

Finally then, here is a summary of some of the key points from the book; I wish you all the best going forward with your increased confidence that you will continue to build based upon your better understanding.

Summary of key points

- There are many factors that affect confidence so ensure you look at all these to get a greater understanding and thus be able to build more confidence and sustain that increased confidence in the long term.

- Consider your thought processes and how they affect your confidence, particularly the 'human' and 'chimp' differences. Learn to manage your chimp, try to act in human mode wherever possible and stick to your core values.

- Make sure you work on doing as many positive and productive things as you can and minimise the negative and unproductive thoughts and behaviours. Positivity breeds more positivity and negativity breeds more negativity so make sure you choose the positive approach.

- You will need to practise and keep practising all the techniques and ways to help build your confidence. The more you practise the easier it will become and the better you will get at it.

- Try to do your best and remember you cannot do better than your best. If you have done your best you should acknowledge it, be happy with that and realise you could not have done anything more.

- Don't worry about failing, as failure is normal. Learn from the experience and learn to deal with any failures in a positive way. Do not fear failure otherwise you will not do those things that can lead to success and more happiness.

- Look to achieve and accomplish things, and when you do, recognise what you have done, be proud and praise yourself. Achieving things and being proud is a sure way of increasing your confidence and will drive you on to achieve even more.

- Look to learn new skills, gain more knowledge and understand more things. Learning creates knowledge and knowledge is power and power increases confidence.

- Recognise those 'gremlins' that you have been living with for so long and see if you can understand them and then get rid of them. The gremlins will not be your fault but you can take responsibility for getting rid of them so they don't continue to burden you.

- It has been said that 'confidence is preparation in action' so where you can, make sure you are prepared. Think, plan and prepare yourself for different situations and it is then more likely you will feel more confident in your ability and then be successful in whatever it is you are going to do.

- Make an effort to smile and laugh more. If you smile at people you will normally get a smile back; it feels good to smile and even better to get that reciprocated. Allow yourself to laugh more, do things that will make you smile and laugh and learn to laugh at yourself too.

- Try to get the right people around you and get rid of the wrong ones. Easier said than done, but it will make such a difference to your happiness, confidence and stress levels. You do have choices and you can make choices about who you want in your life and who you don't.

- Do more of the things you enjoy doing and do them more often. It is too easy to get bogged down with life and the negative things that are going on, but remember you only live once and you have to make efforts to enjoy it. So think about those things that you enjoy and look to make them happen more often.

- Be nice to yourself (and your chimp). Often people will beat themselves up about all kinds of things, maybe feel guilty and maybe even seek to punish themselves in some way. Also, when your chimp plays up it often gets told off or punished in an unpleasant way. Learn to be nicer to yourself and your chimp. Be reassuring to your chimp, give yourself some 'you' time, give yourself a break and treat yourself how you would hope to be treated.

- Don't compare so much and never be jealous. Nothing good can come from jealousy and the green-eyed monster as it is so negative and unproductive. Whenever you feel yourself making comparisons or getting jealous you must stop.

Recognise what you are doing and remind yourself it is not just a waste of time but very damaging to yourself.

- And finally remember that the vast majority of people are a lot less confident than you think! They will have issues, insecurities, worries, fears and all kinds of problems. They may be good at covering it up or they may be good with dealing with those issues but nobody is immune to problems. The key is to focus on how you can deal with issues, how you can feel more confident and ultimately how you can be happier.

About the
'Climb Your Mountain' Charity

Climb Your Mountain (CYM) was set up as a charity in 2008 with the aim of helping anyone who is going through a difficult time in their life by supporting them in climbing their own personal mountain. It is for anybody, any age, any background and recognises that stress, depression, low confidence, health issues, associated conditions and lack of general wellbeing can be damaging and can affect anybody for many different reasons.

The charity has two main focuses. Firstly, there is an emphasis on using physical exercise and activities as a way of dealing with, managing, preventing and treating issues. There is a wide range of benefits to physical exercise and activities yet it is often hard to motivate yourself, especially when you are feeling low. Also, many people are not aware of the huge benefits that physical exercise and activities can have on their mental health and wellbeing as well as their physical health.

So the charity provides many opportunities as well as encouragement and motivation for people to do more exercise and take part in more physical activities. Hundreds of free organised walks, hikes, runs, climbs and cycle rides across the country, in a friendly and safe environment, take place each year. Anyone can participate and people are there to benefit from enjoying the activities, meeting new people, seeing new places and becoming healthier and happier.

The second focus is on education and providing information and knowledge for people about physical and mental health and overall wellbeing. CYM offers free educational courses and workshops that cover a wide range of topics including stress and depression (symptoms, causes, prevention, management and treatment), anxiety, brain chemistry, food and mood, benefits of exercise, confidence and self-esteem, motivation, and barriers to wellbeing. The range of self-help books expand on the course content and can reach more people, offering practical help and advice so that they are in a better position to help themselves and to be able to help others.

To find out more about the 'Climb Your Mountain' charity:

Website www.climbyourmountain.org

Email info@climbyourmountain.org

We rely heavily for funding on people making donations and raising money from taking part in trips and challenges. If you can help by making a donation please go to

www.justgiving.com/climbym

or get in touch and take part in a trip or challenge with us!

You can also TEXT a £5 donation to the charity

TEXT: BOOK32£5

To: 70070

Or an online donation via:

www.justgiving.com/healthbooks

THANK YOU!